THE HARVEST JUST AHEAD

by Derek Prince

Books by Derek Prince

Appointment in Jerusalem
Atonement: Your Appointment
  with God
Blessing or Curse: You Can Choose
Called to Conquer
Choice of a Partner, The
Complete Salvation
Declaring God's Word
Derek Prince—A Biography by
  Stephen Mansfield
Derek Prince: On Experiencing
  God's Power
Destiny Of Israel and The Church,
Divine Exchange, The
Does Your Tongue Need Healing?
End of Life's Journey, The
Entering the Presence of God
Expelling Demons
Explaining Blessings and Curses
Extravagant Love
Faith to Live By
Fasting
First Mile, The
Foundations For Christian Living
Gateway to God's Blessing
Gifts of the Spirit, The
God Is a Matchmaker
God's Medicine Bottle
God's Plan for Your Money
God's Remedy for Rejection
God's Will for Your Life
God's Word Heals
Grace of Yielding, The
Harvest Just Ahead, The
Holy Spirit in You, The
How to Fast Successfully
Husbands and Fathers
I Forgive You

Judging
Life's Bitter Pool
Lucifer Exposed
Marriage Covenant, The
Orphans, Widows, the Poor and
  Oppressed
Our Debt to Israel
Pages from My Life's Book
Partners for Life
Philosophy, the Bible and the
  Supernatural
Power in the Name
Power of the Sacrifice, The
Prayers and Proclamations
Praying for the Government
Protection from Deception
Promise of Provision, The
Promised Land
Prophetic Guide to the End Times
Receiving God's Best
Rediscovering God's Church
Rules of Engagement
Secrets of a Prayer Warrior
Self-Study Bible Course (revised
  and expanded)
Set Apart For God
Shaping History Through Prayer
  and Fasting
Spiritual Warfare
Surviving the Last Days
They Shall Expel Demons
Through the Psalms with Derek
  Prince
War in Heaven
Who Is the Holy Spirit?
You Matter to God
You Shall Receive Power

THE HARVEST JUST AHEAD

by Derek Prince

THE HARVEST JUST AHEAD

ISBN 978-1-908594-01-3
Product Code: B111

Scripture quotations are from the New King James Version of the Bible, Thomas Nelson Publishers, Nashville, TN, © 1982.

This book was compiled from the extensive archive of Derek Prince's unpublished materials and edited by the Derek Prince Ministries editorial team.

INTRODUCTION
TO
THE HARVEST JUST AHEAD

As near as we can determine, the core of this message, "The Harvest Just Ahead," was delivered extemporaneously by Derek Prince sometime in the mid-1970s, presumably to an audience of college-age young people. It is one of the most compelling calls we have ever heard for workers in the end-time harvest—a harvest that will be taking place in the days ahead.

We believe "The Harvest Just Ahead" is a direct challenge to each of us from the Holy Spirit of God, spoken through our friend, mentor and Bible teacher, Derek Prince.

In fact, halfway through his original presentation, Derek stated that he knew it was the Lord who had prompted him to speak on the theme of the Harvest. He candidly informed his audience that "not one sentence" of what he was sharing appeared in the outline of his prepared notes for his message that day.

Then Derek added: "I'm forced to the conclusion that God had me say today what I have said to you. And in the light of that, I have the obligation to bring you to a place of choice."

As you read this booklet, we believe the Lord will bring you as well to a place of choice. So, please read, absorb, and then make a firm decision to present yourself to the Lord. Prepare to give yourself, without reservation, to the Lord of the Harvest as a worker He will use to bring multitudes of people into His Kingdom in these significant days.

– The International Publishing Team
Derek Prince Ministries

THE HARVEST JUST AHEAD

The Bible tells us that no one knows the day or the hour of the Lord's coming, but I believe it's very close. I'm not saying Jesus will come in this millennium, but I think He will come sooner than most of us expect. However, the events of His coming will happen in divine order, as God has outlined for us in Scripture. First will come the latter rain (the outpouring of the Holy Spirit), then the harvest (the final ingathering of souls), and finally, the coming of the Lord Jesus.

I sense that the Holy Spirit of God is very much in earnest about this particular message, "The Harvest Just Ahead." Perhaps that is because it is an urgent call to every Christian, but especially to the Christians of America, to be involved in this glorious task of reaping the harvest, so that He can come for His Bride, the Church.

I believe I have a unique perspective for this nation because, although I am an American, I am originally from Great Britain. But as I deliver this message to the people of the great nation of the United States, it is not as a Britisher, but as an American speaking to Americans. So to begin, I would like to share with you a brief history of how I came to be a citizen of the United States.

In 1963, God sovereignly intervened in my life and called me to America. I came to the United States for what was supposed to be a temporary, six-month visit. However, the Lord had other plans, and in July of 1970, I became an American citizen. I have counted that citizenship a privilege ever since.

I was deeply proud of my British citizenship, and therefore it was a major decision to renounce it in order to become a citizen of the United States. But I had a deep assurance that I was in the will of God.

I was born a Britisher, born into the British Empire when it was at its height. My whole family was what you would call "Empire Builders," officers of the British army in India, where I was born.

And in my lifetime, I have seen a complete empire crumble and fall.

One truth I have learned is that political and

military powers are not permanent. They must be conserved and guarded, and conditions must be met if a nation is going to retain them.

It isn't easy for British people to acknowledge that the leadership of the world passed from them to the United States, but the destiny of nations is in God's hands. So why, in His providence, did God allow Britain to decline? And why did He allow America to advance?

I believe God brought forth this country, with its unique privileges, its unique wealth, its unique potentiality, not only to lead the free world, but for a purpose yet to be fulfilled; that out of the seed of God's Word that gave birth to this great nation, there is to develop an army that will go forth and reap the harvest.

That is why this message, "The Harvest Just Ahead," is weighted with such a sense of urgency and importance. In our modern world we have a repetition of the situation in Jesus' own day, when Jesus looked out on the multitudes and said, "The harvest is plentiful, but the workers [to gather in the harvest] are few" (Matthew 9:37 NIV).

As a nation, we stand at the crossroads of our destiny in God and our current path into decline. Are we going to obey the true and living God as our forefathers did, and go forth and reap the harvest? Or are we going to reject God and His purposes, and ultimately perish in disaster and defeat?

God gives nations a choice. And my message to the church of Jesus Christ in America is this: we must choose to serve the Lord faithfully and diligently as labourers in "The Harvest Just Ahead."

The Great Ingathering

What is the harvest? In the spiritual sense, it is the last, great ingathering of people from all nations, all over the world, into God's kingdom at the close of this age. It is the result of much work, much sowing, much labour, much sacrifice, and much planning. But ultimately the harvest cannot happen unless God sends the "latter rain," which is the outpouring of the Holy Spirit.

Being born into a military family, I have never been much of a farmer. I did, however, spend six months in southern Ireland at the beginning of World War II working on a farm, looking after sheep, mending gaps in hedges, separating milk and doing other similar chores. Although my basic knowledge of farming is quite limited, I learned enough to say this: there is a climax to which everything moves forward in agriculture. That climax is the harvest. Everything that is done is done for the sake of the harvest.

This is also true in the spiritual realm. The harvest is the primary purpose to which all other activities of God are directed. Jesus Himself points this out in a simple but important statement He makes in Matthew 13:39. As part of the interpretation of the parable of the wheat and the tares He says, "The harvest is the end of the age."

It is very important to bear this in mind. The harvest is the end of the age. This age is building to a climax, and the climax is the harvest. Basically, all the events and processes that have happened in the Church for nearly two thousand years have been ultimately directed toward this climax: the harvest.

WAITING FOR HIS COMING

There are many events that have to take place before the harvest can be gathered in. I want to mention one in particular in James 5:7 and 8:

Therefore be patient, brethren, until the coming of the Lord. See how the farmer waits for the precious fruit of the earth, waiting patiently for it until it receives the early and latter rain. You also be patient. Establish your hearts, for the coming of the Lord is at hand.

Notice, the farmer does not gather in the harvest until he has received both the early and latter rain. All of this is directly related to the coming of the Lord. It is in the period of the restoration of all things that we can look for the personal return of the Lord Jesus Christ.

But first, there must be the harvest, which synchronizes with the coming of the Lord. The two are inseparably united. At the end of the harvest, the Lord will come, and James tells us we must be patient.

THE PURPOSE OF THE RAIN

The essence of all Bible teaching about rain is that it is given for the sake of the harvest. I want to emphasize to you that this is a very important principle that runs all through the Word of God. Rain is always given for the sake of the harvest.

We know from many Scriptures that the former rain and the latter rain are biblical pictures of the outpouring of the Holy Spirit. The church age began with a major outpouring of the Holy Spirit, and it is closing with a major outpouring of the Holy Spirit. If we do not realize that the outpouring of the Holy Spirit is given for the sake of the harvest, we will miss the purposes of God.

A PICTURE OF DESOLATION AND RESTORATION

For a more in-depth understanding of God's plan for the restoration of all things, let's turn to the book of Joel. Joel is the great prophet of this latter day outpouring of the Holy Spirit we are experiencing.

The three chapters that comprise the book of Joel have a theme that unfolds very simply and can be stated in three words, corresponding to those chapters: 1) desolation, 2) restoration and 3) judgment.

Chapter one of Joel is a picture of desolation in every area of the inheritance of God's people. Chapter two of Joel contains the gracious promise of restoration in verse 25, "I will restore to you the years that the swarming locust has eaten, the crawling locust, the consuming locust, and the chewing locust." Chapter three of Joel is the warning of judgment upon those who reject restoration.

As we first focus on the desolation and restoration described in chapters one and two, there are two symbolic trees in the forefront of Joel's imagery which are types, or pictures, of God's people. The first tree is the fig tree, which is Israel, God's people by natural descent from Abraham. The other tree is the vine, which is the Church, God's people brought about by spiritual birth, born again of the Spirit of God through faith in Jesus Christ.

So the fig tree and the vine—Israel and the Church—find themselves in the desolation described in chapter 1, verse 12:

> *The vine has dried up, and the fig tree has withered; . . . all the trees of the field*

are withered; surely joy has withered away from the sons of men.

Through the invasion of locusts and drought, there can be no harvest and therefore no offerings to the Lord of grain, new wine and oil;

The field is wasted, the land mourns; for the grain is ruined, the new wine is dried up, the oil fails. Be ashamed, you farmers, wail, you vinedressers, for the wheat and the barley; because the harvest of the field has perished.

Joel 1:10–11

RESTORATION BEGINS WITH RAIN

But in the second chapter of Joel we have the full promise of restoration to both the fig tree and the vine, representing both Israel and the Church. We find that it is presented in prophetic symbolism as a promise of rain, beginning with verse 23:

Be glad then, you children of Zion, and rejoice in the LORD your God; for He has given you the former rain faithfully, and He will cause the rain to come down for you—the former rain, and the latter rain in the first month. The threshing floors shall be full of wheat, and the vats shall overflow with new wine and oil. "So I will restore to you the years that the swarming locust has eaten, the crawling locust, the consuming locust, and the chewing locust, My great army which I sent among you. You shall eat in plenty and be satisfied, and praise the name of the LORD your God, who has dealt wondrously with you; and My people shall never be put to shame. Then you shall know that I am in the midst of Israel: I am the LORD your God and there is no other. My people shall never be put to shame."

Joel 2:23–27

What is God's solution? It begins with the first or former rain, the first great major outpouring of rain that falls in Israel. Usually that rain comes in November at the end of the dry season and it heralds the beginning of the cold winter season. It is universal, it is heavy, and it is dramatic. Its purpose is to soften the soil, which by then is baked hard, so that the farmer can begin the various processes that are going to lead up to next year's harvest.

After that, through the cold winter months—November, December, January, and February—rain will continue to fall. But it will fall unpredictably, sporadically, in little outpourings here and there. There will be no further major, overall outpouring of rain until the end of the winter season.

In Joel 2:23, the verse just cited, it says "the first month." Remember that when Israel came out of Egypt during the first Passover, that month became the first month of the year.

> *Now the LORD spoke to Moses and Aaron in the land of Egypt, saying, "This month shall be your beginning of months; it shall be the first month of the year to you."*
>
> *Exodus 12:1–2*

Passover coincides more or less with Christianity's Easter. So at the end of the winter, in the "first month" (which in the land of Israel is April) God sends the latter, or the last, rain. This marks the close of the winter season, and the beginning of the dry season. It is the greatest, heaviest, most widespread outpouring of rain in Israel that takes place at any time in the year. In the economy of God, its agricultural purpose is to germinate the seed that has been sown. After that, events move very rapidly into the process of gathering in the harvest.

Again we see a principle that runs all through the Bible: rain is always given for the sake of the harvest. We need to understand the pattern of rainfall in Israel, because the moving of the Holy Spirit in the Church is represented by the way rain falls in Israel.

Beginning in Deuteronomy chapter 11 at verse 10 and then onward, we find a promise God makes to His people. He promises that if they would obey Him and walk in His Word, He would send them the rain that they might gather in the harvest.

> *"For the land which you go to possess is not like the land of Egypt from which you have come, where you sowed your seed and watered it by foot, as a vegetable garden; but the land which you cross over to possess is a land of hills and valleys, which drinks water from the rain of heaven, a land for which the Lord your God cares; the eyes of the Lord your God are always on it, from the beginning of the year to the very end of the year. 'And it shall be that if you earnestly obey My commandments which I command you today, to love the Lord your God and serve Him with all your heart and with all your soul, then I will give you the rain*

*for your land in its season, the early rain
[or the former rain] and the latter rain,
[And then notice the purpose in God's
economy:] that you may gather in your
grain, your new wine, and your oil.'"*
Deuteronomy 11:10–14

Notice that rain is a gift from God. The Bible
emphasizes that rain is under the sovereign
control of the Lord.

THE PATTERN IN CHURCH HISTORY

Let's now apply this prophetic picture to the
pattern of church history. The church age began
at Pentecost with the first rain, the former rain.
It was the first great, dramatic outpouring of the
Holy Spirit. With this I think almost all theologians
and historians would agree.

When questioned about the outpouring taking
place, Peter immediately identified it with Joel's
prophecy, saying:

*"But this is what was spoken by the
prophet Joel:*

*'And it shall come to pass in the last
days, says God, that I will pour out of
My Spirit on all flesh; your sons and your
daughters shall prophesy, your young
men shall see visions, your old men shall*

dream dreams. And on My menservants
and on My maidservants I will pour out
My Spirit in those days; and they shall
prophesy.'"

Acts 2:16–18

But you will notice that Peter goes on to the
close of the age, relaying what the Lord says He
will do then:

"'I will show wonders in heaven
above and signs on the earth beneath:
Blood and fire and vapour of smoke. The
sun shall be turned into darkness, and
the moon into blood, before the coming
of the great and awesome day of the LORD.
And it shall come to pass that whoever
calls on the name of the LORD s h a l l   b e
saved.'"

Acts 2:19–21

So we see that Peter took that prophecy right
up to the close of this age. People say, "Well,
isn't that strange? Because that was nearly two
thousand years ago, and the age hasn't closed."

But it is not strange at all, because Peter was
quoting from Joel. And Joel said the Spirit will
come to the Church in two major outpourings—
the former rain at the beginning of the church
age and the latter rain to close the church age,

corresponding to the climate of Israel.

What we are living in today is the latter rain—the last great, universal, heaviest outpouring of the Holy Spirit that will ever come in the history of the human race. I believe we are living in that day. If that rain had not been given, the harvest could not be gathered in.

Two Kinds of People

So again we ask: What is the harvest? It is the great ingathering of people into the Kingdom of God. Bear this in mind, because this is an answer leading up to the question that we are going to deal with next. Here is the question: How can I become effective as a result of the outpouring of the Holy Spirit in my life? The answer is, by linking up with God's purpose.

There are two kinds of people who get the baptism of the Holy Spirit, and there have been all through the years. There are those who have understood the reason for the outpouring and there are those who have not understood that reason.

Those who have not understood are filled with the Spirit and keep it to themselves. They become, in too many cases, super-spiritual little "Bless-Me" clubs. They meet, prophesy to one another, lay hands on one another, and have visions and revelations. Then they say, "God bless you, brother. It's been great to be together. See you the same time next week." And two years later they have neither grown nor decreased. They are just the same. They haven't grasped the purpose of God.

I want to say this with all the emphasis at my command: The rain is given for the sake of the harvest. It is not given to make you super-spiritual or especially blessed. The rain of the Holy Spirit is given to make you an effective worker in God's harvest.

The rain isn't given for the sake of the rain itself. The rain is given for the sake of the harvest. And there are other people with no better education, no better seminary training than anyone else who have received the baptism of the Holy Spirit and turned the world upside down. Why? Because they realize that the power of the Spirit has been given to them for the sake of the harvest, the ingathering of souls.

The rain of the Spirit is not given to make us super-spiritual. It is given us to gather in the harvest.

FOR THE SAKE OF THE HARVEST

Throughout its entirety, the Bible speaks about the harvest with great emphasis. If we look at the various significant festivals of Mosaic Law and the covenant, we find that every one of them has its corresponding event in the Christian era. Passover, for instance, coincides with Easter; the Feast of the Harvest, with Pentecost; and so on. I firmly believe that these links apply to the harvest, and that the harvest will have its fulfillment.

There is going to be a specific period in the history of the Church which is the harvest period. And I believe it is directly linked to the latter rain. But I believe it is also linked to another fascinating feature of the days in which we live: the population explosion. As I understand it, the population of the earth is going to be doubling every sixty years from this point onward. There were well over 6.5 billion people in the earth in 2009, and it won't be long before there will be 7 billion, 8 billion, and more. Whether they are correct or not, experts are warning us there won't be enough food to eat and there won't be enough land to live on.

I believe without a doubt that God knew all along about the population explosion. And I believe He has a purpose for it. Let me suggest it to you this way: if the programme of Joel is carried out, if the Church is purged of its duplicity and immaturity, if the Church is filled afresh with the Holy Spirit, experiencing divine unction and power, if the Church is gathered out of its little corners and sects and from behind its little barriers and becomes one again in Jesus Christ, such a Church could go forth into the world today in the power of the Holy Spirit. And going forth in power, the Church could see more souls saved in the world in a few years than have been saved in all the years from the time of Jesus until today.

This is the harvest, and it lies just ahead. The latter rain is being given for the sake of the harvest. God is already beginning to put His hand on people, saying, "Get ready now. Get loosed. Get detached. Because when the harvest comes, it is going to be so quick that you will have to be ready to cast in the sickle and reap."

Like Lightning

In the year 1948 or 1949, the Latter Rain movement broke out in Canada. (And by the way, that was a real move of God.) During that movement, a young girl in the city of Edmonton or Calgary had a vision of this latter day revival, and she saw the last harvest. In her vision, she said it was just like lightning that circled the earth quickly, and then it was over. This is how it is going to be. It will be as quick as lightning.

In the book of Jeremiah, we see Jeremiah rebuking the people of his day in Israel because they were not aware of what God was doing. They were wrapped up in themselves, in their own carnal concerns. They were blind and deaf to what God was saying and doing. He says:

"This people has a defiant and rebel-

lious heart; they have revolted and de-
parted [from God. What is the evidence?]
They do not say in their heart, 'Let us
now fear the LORD our God, who gives
rain, both the former and the latter, in its
season. He reserves for us the appointed
weeks of the harvest.'"

Jeremiah 5:23–24

Notice that the rain is given for the sake of the harvest. What was the mistake that Israel made? They did not realize that they were totally dependent on God for the rain and that the rain was given for the sake of the harvest. They missed God's purpose. God reserves the appointed weeks of the harvest.

That became a startling revelation to me some years ago. Actually, I had walked into a restaurant a little earlier and selected a table where I wanted to sit. But when I went over to sit down, there was a little sign on the table that showed me I could not sit there. Guess what it was. RESERVED. And when I read this passage I thought, *That's it!* God has put a little sign over just a few short weeks in which the harvest has to be gathered in. He's reserved it. He said to Satan, "You can't have those weeks. I've set them apart for the harvest." Not months, but weeks. If you are a farmer or one who works the land, you realize that the most critical, busiest season of the year is the harvest, when everybody has to be sent out.

God is warning His people all the time—it's coming quickly, it's coming quickly. There has been a long, slow process of maturing and preparation. But when the harvest comes, friend, if you are not ready you will not even know it has happened. It is going to come that quickly.

ACCEPTING THE VISITATION

Let's look once more at Jeremiah 5:23 and 24, which shows how God's people missed the significance of the rain God provided for the harvest.

> *"But this people has a defiant and rebellious heart; they have revolted and departed. They do not say in their heart, 'Let us now fear the LORD our God, who gives rain, both the former and the latter, in its season. He reserves for us the appointed weeks of the harvest.'"*

It is important for us to recognize that it is a very terrible step to reject what God is doing when He gives the rain. Those ministers and groups and churches who will not see what God is doing, who reject this move of the Holy Spirit, have a "defiant and rebellious heart." They have "revolted and departed." I'm not saying this to attack anybody, nor am I seeking to please anybody.

Let me tell you what I believe. I believe we are presently seeing God's last offer of mercy to the United States of America. If the Christians of America do not respond to God, there is nothing ahead but desolation and judgment for this nation.

I believe it is life or death, friends. And that is why I don't compromise when I speak about it. I believe it can be life. I believe God loves the United States, and that He set this nation apart in destiny for something special. But I tremble to think what will happen to this nation if in the next few years it does not accept this divine visitation of the Holy Spirit.

Do you know why atheistic communism came to Russia? Because there was a visitation of the Holy Spirit in the 1870s and 1880s, and the Russian Christians rejected it. When they rejected the Holy Spirit, they created a spiritual vacuum which was automatically filled by the next most powerful spirit in the world, and that is the spirit of antichrist.

The spirit of antichrist is at work everywhere in the United States, in our campuses and colleges and in our churches and seminaries. There is coming a fearful moment of climax when we must decide: Is it going to be Christ or antichrist? There is no third alternative.

A Sobering Choice

Israel came to that place nineteen centuries ago: "Which of the two do you want me to release to you?" Pilate asked, "Jesus or Barabbas?" (See Matthew 27:21.) Israel didn't have a third choice. Fools that they were, they said, "Not this man [Jesus], but Barabbas." They chose Barabbas, even though he was an agitator, a man of violence, and a professional protester.

Have you ever considered the two responses the Jewish people made? First they said, "Not this man, but Barabbas." (See Luke 23:18.) Then Pilate said to them, "What then shall I do with your King Jesus?" Their reply? "We have no king but Caesar." (See John 19:15.) They denied the Lord as their King.

If you read nineteen centuries of Jewish history, what do you see as you read? Caesar and Barabbas ruling over the Jewish people. What they chose they got. When God tells you to choose, you have to choose. And you get what you choose.

How many Caesars, how many emperors, how many kings, how many dictators have persecuted and oppressed the Jewish nation in nineteen centuries? How many times did those Caesars take Barabbas, the professional agitator, the man of violence, the rabble-rouser, and turn him against the Jews? Do you know Jewish history? Again and again and again.

The last horrific example was Adolf Hitler and the Nazi Storm Troopers. Do you know what Hitler's philosophy was? It was based on the chilling philosophy of a man named Spengler whose teaching was, "We need another Caesar."

GOD'S HOUR OF DECISION

When I come to this point in my presentation (and frankly, I did not plan to come to such a sobering point), I am gripped by the awful solemnity of choice. Nineteen centuries ago Israel made a choice, given to them by God. They got what they chose, exactly down to the minutest detail.

Today the choice is America's. "Which of the two, Jesus or Barabbas?" Our country is filled with violence, riots, hatred, strife—it is ripe for Barabbas. But you have a choice. You have a choice. This is God's hour of choice. This is God's hour of visitation. This is not a little church parlour game. This is death or life. I believe it can be life.

I absolutely believe that God desires to send to the United States of America the greatest revival in the history of this or any nation. I haven't come to that belief by accident. For years I've prayed over it, meditated on it, fasted and sought God concerning it. I am convinced that I speak the truth from Almighty God. I'm not normally a particularly bold or self-assertive type of person, but I have a deep, inner conviction that I am speaking to you a message from God.

I will not compromise about divine truth, because I will have to answer to God one day for what I say. There are many places in the Bible where God tells men and women to choose. In Deuteronomy 30:19, Moses said:

"I call heaven and earth as witnesses today against you, that I have set before you life and death, blessing and cursing; therefore choose life, that both you and your descendants may live."

Do you know what thought has gripped me? The idea that God lets man choose. God has set before us this simple choice—you can have life and blessing, or you can have death and cursing. Moses said, "I advise you to choose life."

Do you know what I have done? I have chosen life, and I have chosen blessing. I am absolutely convinced that I will get what I have chosen, just as Israel got what they chose when they made the wrong choice.

About one generation later, Joshua said, "Choose for yourselves this day whom you will serve" (Joshua 24:15). Notice that the choice was not "whether." Many people think, "I can choose if I'll serve God or the devil, or I can simply choose to please myself."

You don't have that choice. The choice is

whether you will serve God or the devil. It's as simple as that. If you say, "Brother Prince, I don't know whom I'm serving," then you are serving the devil. Those who serve God walk in the light and they know whom they are serving.

Elijah came to Israel a few generations later and said, "If the LORD is God, serve Him; but if Baal, serve him. But make your minds up and do it quickly." (See 1 Kings 18:21.)

WHO WILL YOU SERVE?

I believe for the Christians of America the time has come to make up your minds. You may say, "My denomination doesn't teach this." You may say, "My church doesn't preach this." Will you build your faith on that flimsy foundation?

What does God ask? He asks that we sell out to Him. He asks that we commit ourselves to Him without reservation, to do His will, to serve Him, to believe and preach His Word. God wants you without reservations, without strings attached. He wants you for His purposes. There is one simple condition to be part of this last great move of God. We don't need to complicate it. It is simple. It is this, and this alone—a total, unreserved commitment to the Lord Jesus Christ. That is all that is required. All the rest will follow from that.

I believe God sent me to tell American Christians that it is time to wake up. The

Christians of the United States do not need to lose the spiritual battle. They can win it. And if you win it, your country will be saved and your land will be healed. If you lose it, it will be to your everlasting discredit.

I don't attack any denomination, or any section of the church. That's not the point. The point is this: What place does Jesus Christ have in your life? The church has one Lord. It's Jesus. The Church has one Head. It's Jesus.

Let me tell you the decision I've made. As far as I'm concerned I belong to the Lord Jesus Christ, spirit, soul and body, for time and eternity. Jesus redeemed me by His blood when He died on the cross and I have given myself to Him. Can you say the same? If you cannot, would you make that decision right now?

The Harvest Is Beginning

The harvest lies ahead. I can't tell you exactly when it will happen, but it is already beginning to ripen in certain areas of the earth. I will tell you the same thing I told the people of Africa some years ago. I said to them, "The harvest is right at your door, and God is going to need workers by the hundreds to cast in the sickle of His Word and reap." The time has come to reap, for the harvest of the earth is ripe.

Jeremiah 8:20 says, "The harvest is past, the

summer is ended, and we are not saved!" When the harvest is past and the summer has ended, there is no more salvation. Then the door is closed.

What about it? What are you living for? What does life mean to you? Paul said, "For to me, to live is Christ" (Philippians 1:21). Jesus is enough. You don't need Christ plus something. You just need Jesus Christ. Our Lord said, "I am the resurrection and the life" (John 11:25). He also said, "I have come that they may have life, and that they may have it more abundantly" (John 10:10).

When you are committed to Jesus Christ, life is rich, it is full, it is exciting, and it is fascinating. I was a professor in a university and I could have been a professor today. But I made a choice. When the Lord called me to preach the gospel, I said, "Yes!" In the eyes of the world, I gave up an excellent position with tremendous possibilities and academic distinctions. But I can say confidently that if I had to face the same decision today I would make the very same choice.

My life has been full. It has been rich. It has been wonderful. I'm not sorry that I dedicated my life to Jesus Christ. I'm only sorry for the times I wasn't fully dedicated, that's all.

Perhaps you want to make a total dedication of your life to the Lord Jesus Christ. Listen, this doesn't mean you are never going to sin again. It doesn't mean that you are never going to have problems. It doesn't mean that you are never going to fail. But it means that you have made a commitment which will keep you when the going gets tough. What I am talking about is a firm, total commitment to Jesus Christ, the Lord of the Harvest, to be a labourer in the harvest fields. When you commit yourself to Jesus Christ, He will tell you the next thing you need to do.

A Prayer of Commitment

If you are somewhat perplexed, confused, uncertain, and you don't have that deep, settled peace and stability in your Christian experience, I want to suggest to you that perhaps the reason is a lack of total commitment. In light of what I have shared in this message, perhaps you would like to make a definite commitment to Jesus Christ right now. Why not tell Him now that you will follow Him for the rest of time and for all eternity? Why not tell Him now that your life is going to be at His disposal for Him to use for His glory by the Holy Spirit in any way He wants?

If it is your desire to make that commitment of the rest of your life to Jesus Christ, then this is my prayer for you. Please pray this prayer now.

Father, in the name of Jesus, I love You and I thank You that I can stand before You as one of Your people who desires to consecrate my life to Jesus Christ.

Lord, I take my stand in my authority as a believer in Jesus Christ, and I loose myself now from every bond, from every fetter, everything that would hold me back from this commitment to Jesus. I declare myself loosed in the name of Jesus and I put myself into Your hand, Lord.

I put myself at Your disposal. You are the Lord of the harvest. You are the Head over all things of the Church which is Your body, and we are Your members. Lord, let me know from this moment onwards that I have come under Your control and that You are going to bless me and strengthen me and use me.

Lord, I pray for the harvest. You said, "Therefore, pray the Lord of the harvest to send out labourers into His harvest."

Lord, I pray that according to Your will, as You see fit, in each circumstance and situation and need, that You will thrust me forth into the harvest field to be a labourer for You, Lord. I pray this in Jesus' name. Amen.

Epilogue

After Derek delivered this powerful message on the harvest, there was a time of praise and worship followed by a very sobering prophetic word brought by Derek Prince.

"Behold, I give unto you power. Unto you I give power. Not unto a past generation, not unto a future generation, but unto you who are hearing this message, I give power according to My Word to tread on serpents and scorpions and over all the power of the enemy. I require you to be endued with power. I require you to be filled with My divine dynamite.

"I require servants who are faithful and obedient, servants who do not run their own errands and go their own ways and deliver their own messages. But I require servants who will stand before Me, the Lord of Hosts, and hear My voice and speak My word.

"For if you will speak My word, you will turn this people away from their sins and you will deliver them from their destructions. But if you will speak your dreams and if you will speak your own thoughts and man's wisdom, then

this people shall surely perish. But I will require it at the hands of My witnesses.

"Yes, I will require it at the hands of the preachers. I will require it at the hands of the ministers of this generation who have not declared the truth of God unto a people that needed to hear not man's wisdom, not human institutions, not doctrinal denominational theories, but My word," saith the Lord.

May the Lord give us the strength and the grace to walk in obedience as we move into the harvest just ahead and be faithful labourers in the harvest field.

• • • • •

About the Author

Derek Prince (1915–2003) was born in India of British parents. Educated as a scholar of Greek and Latin at Eton College and Cambridge University, England, he held a Fellowship in Ancient and Modern Philosophy at King's College. He also studied several modern languages, including Hebrew and Aramaic, at Cambridge University and the Hebrew University in Jerusalem.

While serving with the British army in World War II, he began to study the Bible and experienced a life-changing encounter with Jesus Christ. Out of this encounter he formed two conclusions: first, that Jesus Christ is alive; second, that the Bible is a true, relevant, up-to-date book. These conclusions altered the whole course of his life, which he then devoted to studying and teaching the Bible.

Derek's main gift of explaining the Bible and its teaching in a clear and simple way has helped build a foundation of faith in millions of lives. His non-denominational, non-sectarian approach has made his teaching equally relevant and helpful to people from all racial and religious backgrounds.

He is the author of over 50 books, 600 audio and 100 video teachings, many of which have been translated and published in more than 100 languages. His daily radio broadcast is translated into Arabic, Chinese (Amoy, Cantonese, Mandarin, Shanghaiese, Swatow),

Croatian, German, Malagasy, Mongolian, Russian, Samoan, Spanish and Tongan. The radio programme continues to touch lives around the world.

Derek Prince Ministries persists in reaching out to believers in over 140 countries with Derek's teachings, fulfilling the mandate to keep on "until Jesus returns." This is effected through the outreaches of more than 45 Derek Prince offices around the world, including primary work in Australia, Canada, China, France, Germany, the Netherlands, New Zealand, Norway, Russia, South Africa, Switzerland, the United Kingdom and the United States. For current information about these and other worldwide locations, visit www.derekprince.com.

DEREK PRINCE MINISTRIES
OFFICES WORLDWIDE

ASIA/ PACIFIC
DPM–Asia/Pacific
38 Hawdon Street, Sydenham
Christchurch 8023,
New Zealand
T: + 64 3 366 4443
E: admin@dpm.co.nz
W: www.dpm.co.nz and
www.derekprince.in

AUSTRALIA
DPM–Australia
1st Floor, 134 Pendle Way
Pendle Hill
New South Wales 2145, Australia
T: + 612 9688 4488
E: enquiries@derekprince.com.au
W: www.derekprince.com.au

CANADA
DPM–Canada
P. O. Box 8354 Halifax,
Nova Scotia B3K 5M1, Canada
T: + 1 902 443 9577
E: enquiries.dpm@eastlink.ca
W: www.derekprince.org

FRANCE
DPM–France
B.P. 31, Route d'Oupia,
34210 Olonzac,
France
T: + 33 468 913872
E: info@derekprince.fr
W: www.derekprince.fr

GERMANY
DPM–Germany
Schwarzauer Str. 56
D-83308 Trostberg,
Germany
T: + 49 8621 64146
E: IBL.de@t-online.de
W: www.ibl-dpm.net

NETHERLANDS
DPM–Netherlands
P. O. Box 349
1960 AH Heemskerk,
The Netherlands
T: + 31 251 255 044
E: info@nl.derekprince.com
W: www.dpmnederland.nl

NORWAY
P. O. Box 129 Lodderfjord
N-5881, Bergen,
Norway
T: +47 928 39855
E: sverre@derekprince.no
W: www.derekprince.no

SINGAPORE
Derek Prince Publications Pte. Ltd.
P. O. Box 2046 ,
Robinson Road Post Office
Singapore 904046
T: + 65 6392 1812
E: dpmchina@singnet.com.sg
English web: www.dpmchina.org
Chinese web: www.ygmweb.org

SOUTH AFRICA
DPM–South Africa
P. O. Box 33367
Glenstantia 0010 Pretoria
South Africa
T: +27 12 348 9537
E: enquiries@derekprince.co.za
W: www.derekprince.co.za

SWITZERLAND
DPM–Switzerland
Alpenblick 8
CH-8934 Knonau
Switzerland
T: + 41(0) 44 768 25 06
E: dpm-ch@ibl-dpm.net
W: www.ibl-dpm.net

UNITED KINGDOM
DPM–UK
Kingsfield, Hadrian Way
Baldock SG7 6AN
UK
T: + 44 (0) 1462 492100
E: enquiries@dpmuk.org
W: www.dpmuk.org

USA
DPM–USA
P. O. Box 19501
Charlotte NC 28219,
USA
T: + 1 704 357 3556
E: ContactUs@derekprince.org
W: www.derekprince.org